Early Learning Modules

Treasures

STECK-VAUGHN
C O M P A N Y
A Subsidiary of National Education Corporation

Treasures

We have a place we call home.

We learn from our family.

We cook good foods.

We talk to each other.

We read and write.

We share special times.

We remember the past.

We sing and dance.

We wear special clothes.

We share stories.

We make beautiful things.

We go many places.

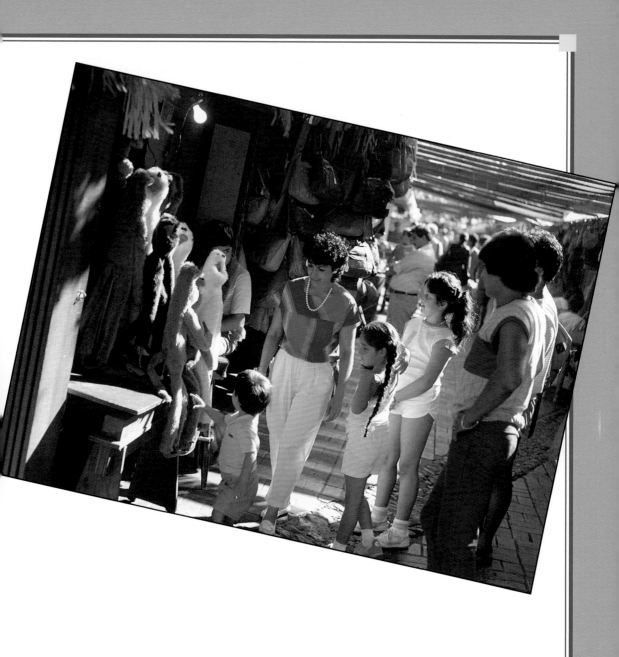

We have fun with friends.

We learn from friends, too!